JANE GOODALL'S ANIMAL WORLD

GORILLAS

by Miriam Schlein

Scientific Consultants: Kelly Stewart and Sandy Harcourt

A Byron Preiss Book

Atheneum   1990   New York

◇ Introduction: The Gorilla by Jane Goodall

I have lived in Africa for thirty years. I have spent hours and hours watching chimpanzees and baboons and all manner of monkeys. But I have not yet seen a wild gorilla, the largest living primate on earth. When I was a child and dreamed of Africa and its forests, I often imagined meeting a group of gorillas. In those days we all thought that they were ferocious creatures who would charge on sight and tear you limb from limb. How wrong we were! It is true that male gorillas may attack humans—but only in defense of their families. On those occasions, they show great courage and often lose their lives as a result.

The only gorilla I have known well was a big male called Guy. He lived in the London Zoo, in the days when the ape house there was like a prison. Guy was kept in solitary confinement in a tiny cage with iron bars and a cement floor. Eventually the zoo decided to give him a young female companion. The first time Guy was allowed to touch her, he lay on his back and put his arms slowly and gently around her and held her close. It was as though he couldn't believe it was really true—that after all those empty years he had a little gorilla to care for. I cried when I watched, it was so moving.

The naturalist George Schaller was the first person to live in the forest near the gorillas. He told us that they were, after all, gentle, shy creatures. And we have learned so much more about them from the life work of the late Dian Fossey, who spent years living among mountain gorillas. Today there are not many mountain gorillas left, but many people are working to save those that remain. The lowland gorillas need our help too, especially in countries where the poaching is very bad indeed.

Let me tell you one last story. It happened at a zoo in England. A little boy, about three years old, fell into the moat around the gorilla enclosure. The big silverback male hurried down to the child, who was unconscious. Everyone thought that this was the end of him. But the huge gorilla picked up the little boy and held him gently, keeping the other curious gorillas away, and then handed him over to his trusted keeper.

Unfortunately, it is we humans who can be the ferocious, destructive primates, not gorillas.

◇ Contents

◇ Where Do Gorillas Live?

Gorillas live in the forests of Africa. The mountain gorilla is found chiefly on the slopes of the Virunga Volcanoes, a mountain range in central Africa that spreads through Rwanda, Uganda, and Zaire. There gorillas roam through the dense, misty forests. They are found at altitudes of up to 12,000 feet.

The lowland gorilla lives in the damp, hot rain forests of Cameroon, Gabon, Congo Brazzaville, the Central African Republic, and Zaire. They avoid clearings and stay in densely wooded areas.

Some forest animals that share the gorilla's habitat are buffalo, elephants, small furry hyraxes, and duikers, a kind of small antelope. The only natural predator of the gorilla is the leopard, which may prey on young or weak gorillas.

It rains a great deal in gorilla territory. Gorillas sometimes take shelter under a tree or sit motionless with arms crossed and head down. When the sun comes out, they seem to enjoy it, and sprawl out to take sunbaths.

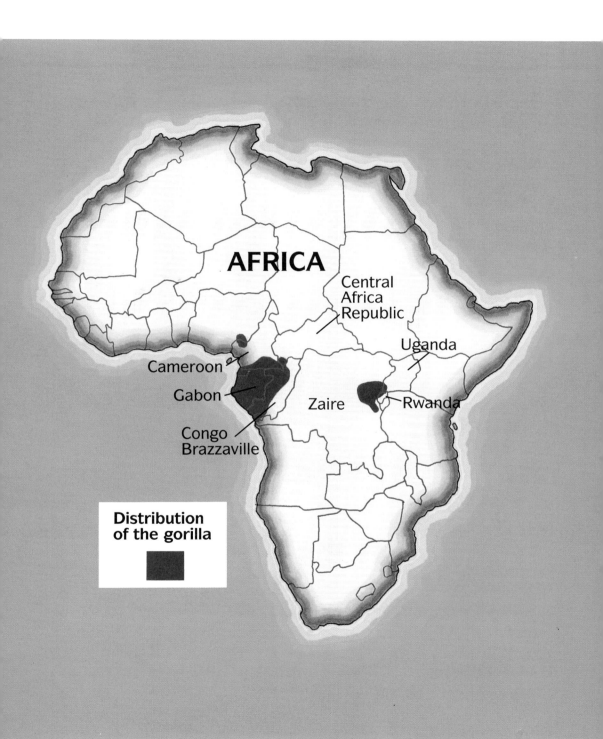

AFRICA

Central
Africa
Republic

Uganda

Cameroon

Gabon

Zaire

Rwanda

Congo
Brazzaville

**Distribution
of the gorilla**

◇ The Family Tree of the Gorilla

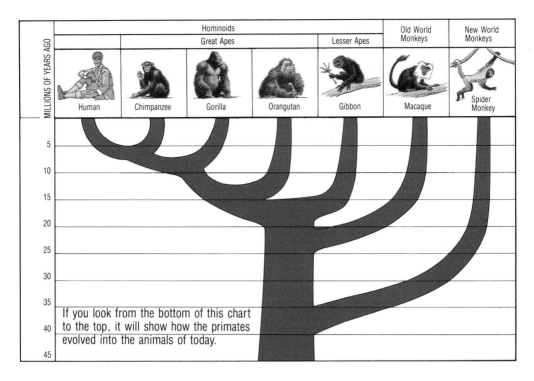

	Hominoids					Old World Monkeys	New World Monkeys
		Great Apes			Lesser Apes		
Human	Chimpanzee	Gorilla	Orangutan		Gibbon	Macaque	Spider Monkey

MILLIONS OF YEARS AGO

5
10
15
20
25
30
35
40
45

If you look from the bottom of this chart to the top, it will show how the primates evolved into the animals of today.

Like other apes, monkeys, and humans, gorillas are in the order (group) of mammals called *primates*. The outstanding characteristic of primates is their large brain. They also have the ability to grasp things. Gorillas are in the family called *Pongidae* (*ponn*-juh-day), which comes from the Kongo word *mpungu*, meaning ape. Other apes are the gibbon, the orangutan, and the chimpanzee.

The first known apelike creatures appeared about twenty-five million years ago. One of these was *Aegyptopithecus* (ay-gip-toe-*pith*-uh-cuss), found in Egypt. During the next ten million years, a variety of apes developed. The remains of one found in Africa and Asia was named *Dryapithecus* (dry-ah-*pith*-uh-cuss). There are two species of Dryapithecus. The larger one evolved into today's gorillas; the medium-sized one

6

evolved into the chimpanzees. The fossil remains of another gorilla, *Gigantopithecus* (ji-gan-toe-*pith*-uh-cuss), was found in China. It lived about a million years ago and was even larger than today's gorillas.

Man is not a descendant of the ape. But we probably share a common ancestor—some apelike creature that lived between twelve and fifteen million years ago.

There is only one species of gorilla. Within this species there are three subspecies—the mountain gorilla *(Gorilla gorilla beringei)*, the eastern lowland gorilla *(Gorilla gorilla graueri)*, and the western lowland gorilla *(Gorilla gorilla gorilla)*. These subspecies differ only slightly in their skull and body structure. The mountain gorilla, because it lives in a colder mountain environment, has longer, thicker hair than the lowland gorilla. It is also a deeper black. The eastern lowland gorilla is the largest.

◇ The Gorilla Community

Gorillas usually live in groups of from twelve to twenty members, though sometimes a group can be larger, with as many as forty, or smaller, with as few as five. Gorilla groups are usually made up of males, females, and young. Some male gorillas live alone and just join up with a group from time to time.

The group is always led by a mature male gorilla called a *silverback*. He gets his name from the silvery-gray hair that first appears on his back when he is eleven or twelve years old. The color sets him apart from the other gorillas, who are totally black. The silverback decides where the group should wander for food, and when and where it should stop to rest. At the end of rest-time the leader gets up and faces in a certain direction. The group knows that this is the way they will be going.

A male gorilla threatens a photographer who is crouching on the ground, but doesn't attack him.

The leader protects the group as well. He does this by means of threats, not violence. He will approach an intruder (either gorilla or human) and just stare. He may stand up, beat his chest, and toss some twigs in the air. If the stranger still doesn't go away, he might rush at him. Still, unless the group is really in danger, the silverback usually doesn't fight. He will either stop short or run right past the intruder.

Until recently, we thought that the gorilla was a fierce, aggressive animal. But in recent years, gorillas have been observed at close range for long periods of time by *ethologists* (scientists who study animal behavior). They have discovered that despite the gorilla's great strength and fierce appearance, it is one of the shyest and gentlest of animals. Only in areas where gorillas have been hunted frequently by humans are male gorillas likely to attack on sight.

Gorillas will not abandon their wounded unless they are forced to. They will defend their young to the death.

◇ Sizing Up the Gorilla

The gorilla is the largest of the great apes. In its normal standing position, resting on its knuckles, its height at the shoulder is about three feet. But if it stands upright, like a human, a gorilla can be more than six feet tall.

Gorillas have broad chests and very long arms. Their outstretched arms can span eight and a half feet—which is more than their height. The average weight of male gorillas is about 400 pounds. Females weigh about 200 pounds.

In a zoo, where he is much less active than in the wild, a male gorilla can weigh 500 pounds or more. In one zoo, a male weighed in at over 750 pounds even after going on a diet!

Measurement: height

Macaque
22 inches

Chimpanzee
4 feet

Baboon
35 inches

Gorilla
5½–6 feet

◇ How the Gorilla Moves

Though gorillas are able to stand upright, they don't walk that way. They walk on all fours—on their feet and on the knuckles of their broad, strong hands. Since their arms are longer than their legs, their backs slope when they walk, so that their strong legs carry most of their weight. Their walking speed is two or three miles an hour. When charging at an intruder, a gorilla will run most of the way on all fours and rise upright for the last few steps of the charge.

Gorillas spend most of the day on the ground, though they sometimes sleep in trees. Young gorillas enjoy swinging from branch to branch. But adult gorillas become too heavy to do this.

Gorillas, like chimpanzees, don't seem to be able to swim. Several times, when zoo gorillas fell into moats surrounding their space, they made no effort to swim, and they drowned.

◇ The Senses of the Gorilla

Gorillas have small ears and small, dark-brown eyes in front of their heads. Scientists think gorillas' eyesight, hearing, and sense of smell are about the same as those of humans.

Gorillas' hands are big, and the thumbs can extend to grasp things. The face, the palms of the hands, and the soles of the feet are hairless.

Gorillas, like the other primates, are highly intelligent.

◇ How Gorillas Communicate

Like other animals, and like people, gorillas often communicate by means of various postures and gestures—what we call *body language*. To a gorilla, staring acts as a threat. A silverback will stare and beat his chest if intruders come too close. Then he may rush toward the intruders, stopping only at the last instant. He may also stand erect and toss twigs and grass up in the air. These are all ways of sending out the message: "Go away."

If a fight is about to erupt between two gorillas, one may crouch on the ground and look down, away from the other. This is the way he says, "I give up."

Gorillas also communicate vocally. They make at least twenty-five different sounds, all meaning different things.

They grunt and roar when they are threatened, and hoot when they are alarmed. They bark when they are curious. A

belchlike sound means they are feeling good. A mother trying to discipline her young makes piglike grunts. And there is a special kind of humming sound gorillas make that is connected with food.

Dian Fossey, a scientist who spent many years observing mountain gorillas, decided to make some of these sounds while she was watching them. First, though, she made sure she knew what the sounds meant to the gorillas. (She did not want to make hostile sounds.) When she hummed, two of the young ones came close to her. Maybe they thought she had some food for them.

Because of the way their vocal cords are formed, gorillas are not able to talk as we do. But Koko, a captive gorilla in San Francisco, has learned to communicate with people using American Sign Language, the system of "signing" used by people who cannot speak or hear. Koko has learned more than 600 signs. She also made up some new signs of her own. When referring to a nut, she called it a "rock fruit." She can say, "Come tickle me." She can also communicate by using a computer. When she presses certain keys, different words are made.

◇ Being Born

Many animals have special breeding seasons, but baby gorillas are born throughout the year. The mother gorilla is pregnant for about eight and a half months. Usually only one baby is born at a time. Gorilla twins are very rare.

At birth, the infant weighs about four and a half pounds. Its skin is chocolate-brown; its fur is shiny black. At first the mother has to hold it to her chest, because it is not strong

enough to cling to her. Soon it can cling to its mother's back and travels "piggyback." When the mother sits, she holds the infant in her arms, so it can nurse. When it rains, she hunches over it to keep it dry, even though she herself is getting soaked.

A mother gorilla will not give birth again for another three and a half to four and a half years. This gives her plenty of time to bring up her baby. The infant needs her love and care while it learns to fend for itself.

◇ Growing Up

Gorilla young are born weak and helpless, but they develop faster than humans. At six weeks of age, the infant gets its first teeth. At about two and a half months it begins to eat plant food—leaves, shoots, and fruit, though it still continues to nurse from its mother.

At three months, the infant gorilla begins to crawl. At four and a half months, it begins walking on all fours. At five or six months, the young gorilla can climb trees. By now it weighs about fifteen pounds.

Young gorillas love to play. They turn somersaults and slide down slopes. They climb trees and swing from branches. They play tag, chasing each other around a group of adults. Sometimes they put crowns of leaves and twigs on their heads for fun. Playing helps young gorillas learn how to get along with others. It also helps build up their strength.

Most of the older gorillas seem to have a good deal of affection for the youngsters in the group. Silverback males often play with them. One big male was seen tickling a gorilla baby with a flower. Sometimes a gorilla "aunt" will babysit for a while. Gorilla mothers need a little time off, too.

A gorilla in the wild may live fifty years.

◇ Living Day to Day

It's seven o'clock in the morning. A group of gorillas is waking up. They don't have to go far for breakfast. Those who made their nests in trees just reach out and grab some leaves from the nearest branches. Some chew on bark. Down on the ground, they break off wild celery stalks or eat thistles. For a while, all you can hear is chewing, branches cracking, and a couple of belches now and then. They eat for a couple of hours. Then they rest.

Often it's misty and rainy where the gorillas live. But today this group is lucky. The weather is fine. They sprawl out on their backs and enjoy the sun.

The group moves on a bit, feeding as they go. They rest again. The young gorillas wrestle and tumble around. Mothers

with small babies groom them, picking ticks out of their fur. When two females start to push each other, quarreling over some piece of fruit, the silverback knuckles over and stares at them. This is enough to stop the argument.

In the early afternoon, the silverback stands up. The others gather around. They walk along a jungle path single file, the leader in front and another male taking up the rear. They travel through a tunnel of underbrush. In a clearing, they pass a couple of buffalo and a forest elephant. The animals pay little attention to one another.

Every so often, when there's something good to eat, the gorillas make a brief stop. Once they pause by a stand of sweet young bamboo and another time at some berry bushes. When it begins to rain, they take shelter under some trees.

The group has walked quite far today—about half a mile. On other days they may go only a few hundred yards. There's no reason to hurry along. Food is all around them.

At about six in the evening, the silverback starts to break branches and make a sleeping nest. The others do the same. Babies share their mothers' nests. Four and five year olds make

their own nests—close to their mothers but separate. The heavy silverback leader and most of the other adult males make their nests on the ground. In some areas, females and young gorillas will make their nests in trees.

In the middle of his task, the silverback looks up. There, off to the side, are three male gorillas—strangers. He takes a few steps toward them and stares. The three aren't doing anything—they're just standing there. The silverback struts back and forth, tossing twigs and grass up into the air. He

beats his chest a few times and roars, then rushes at the intruders—but stops short in front of them. They take the hint and disappear into the rain forest.

While this is going on, the group has remained close together, watching. Now that the confrontation is over, they finish their nest-making. By seven o'clock, the gorillas are bedded down for another night.

The next evening the group will build new nests in a new place. They rarely go back and use their old nests.

◇ Gorillas in Captivity

Animal traders first tried to capture gorillas for zoos in the late 1800s. One trader finally managed (with the help of 800 Africans) to catch two gorillas with nets. When they reached the Hamburg Zoo in Germany, the animals lived only two weeks. According to the zoo director, the gorillas died of homesickness. He was probably right. No one really knew how to care for zoo animals in those days. They were kept alone in a cage, surrounded by bars and cement.

Since then we have learned how to take better care of animals in captivity. Zoo gorillas are now allowed to live in groups, not alone. In many zoos, instead of cement cages, gorillas can live in natural surroundings, with bushes, bamboo, trees, and grass.

There are now more than 600 lowland gorillas in zoos around the world. There are no mountain gorillas in captivity. Many captive gorillas live to an old age. And in 1956, for the first time, a baby gorilla was born in a zoo—a female named Colo, at the zoo in Columbus, Ohio.

We now know that gorilla infants, like human babies, need affection and personal attention. In the wild, young females are able to watch mother gorillas care for their offspring. In a zoo, they do not always have a chance to see this. So, often they don't know how to care for their own infants, especially the firstborn. If this happens, the infant is reared by humans until it is old enough to take care of itself.

One of the most unusual gorillas is Snowflake, who lives at the Barcelona Zoo, in Spain. Snowflake is an *albino* gorilla. This means its skin and hair lack normal color. Pink-skinned and blue-eyed, this white gorilla was found in western Africa. It was clinging to a black gorilla who had been shot and killed.

In the wild, gorillas eat a mostly vegetarian diet. They are often fed differently in zoos. In addition to bananas and apples, Snowflake and his companion Muni eat jelly, ham, roast chicken, yogurt, beef, hardboiled eggs, and cookies.

◇ Protecting the Gorilla

Like other animals, the gorilla lives in a steadily shrinking habitat. Where there were once thick rain forests, there are now farms, grazing lands, and villages. As man's land use expands, the gorillas are forced into smaller and smaller areas.

Between 40,000 and 55,000 lowland gorillas survive in the wild. But the mountain gorilla population is down to about 450. If great effort is not made right now to help them survive, they may be extinct within fifty years.

African nations have set aside large protected areas for gorillas. Parc National des Virungas in Zaire and the Parc National des Volcans in Rwanda spread over the spur of mountains where most remaining mountain gorillas live. In Congo Brazzaville, Zaire, Gabon, and other countries, national parks have been created in rain forests to protect the home of lowland gorillas.

But even in these areas, the gorillas still cannot live undisturbed. Trees in the parks are cut for lumber. Land is mined for minerals. People come in and cut grass for roof-thatch. They let their cattle graze there. They set traps to catch duikers, and sometimes trap a gorilla. And poachers still illegally catch gorilla babies to send to zoos, and kill the adults in order to capture the babies. They also kill them in order to sell parts as "souvenirs." Some people will pay $1,000 for a gorilla head and $600 for a hand! Though guards patrol the parks, they cannot catch all the poachers.

Gorillas, along with chimpanzees, are more like humans than any other animal. They share our emotions. They can laugh and be happy. They can also be sad. They will give up their lives to protect their young. Can we humans be so uncaring as to let them become extinct?

The Mountain Gorilla Project in Rwanda, the Gorilla Conservation Project in Zaire, and the Gorilla and Chimpanzee

30

Station in Gabon have been formed to help the gorilla. But the task cannot be carried out by the African nations alone. People around the world, through their governments and through wildlife organizations, should help provide more funds and people to work to save the gorillas before it is too late—before they disappear forever from the earth.

About the Contributors

JANE GOODALL was born in London on April 3, 1934, and grew up in Bournemouth, on the southern coast of England. In 1960, she began studying chimpanzees in the wild in Gombe, Tanzania. After receiving her doctorate in ethology at Cambridge University, Dr. Goodall founded the Gombe Stream Research Center for the study of chimpanzees and baboons. In 1977, she established the Jane Goodall Institute for Wildlife Research, Education and Conservation to promote animal research throughout the world. She has written three books for adults, including the bestseller *In the Shadow of Man*, and three books for children, including the acclaimed *My Life With the Chimpanzees* and *The Chimpanzee Family Book*.

MIRIAM SCHLEIN is the author of more than sixty books for children. Six of those have been chosen as Junior Literary Guild selections, six others were named as Outstanding Science Books for Children, as selected by the National Science Teachers Association/Children's Book Council Joint Committee. She is the recipient of the Boys Clubs of America Junior Book Medal, and her book *Project Panda Watch* was cited as an Honor Book by the New York Academy of Sciences. She is also the author of *Pandas, Hippos,* and *Elephants* in the Jane Goodall's Animal World series. She is the mother of two grown children and lives in New York City.

Jane Goodall's commitment to the animal world is expressed in her words, "Only when we understand can we care. Only when we care can we help. Only when we help shall they be saved." You can learn more about joining in her efforts to protect endangered wildlife by contacting The Jane Goodall Institute for Wildlife Research, Education and Conservation, P.O. Box 26846, Tucson, Arizona 85726.

Atheneum
Macmillan Publishing Company
866 Third Avenue, New York, NY 10022
Collier Macmillan Canada, Inc.

First Edition

Printed in the United States of America

Cover photo copyright © by Evelyn Gallardo
Back cover photo copyright © by Boyd Norton
Front cover photo insert of Jane Goodall by Hugo Van Lawick, copyright © National Geographic Society
Introduction photo of Jane Goodall copyright © Ben Asen
Interior illustrations copyright © 1990 by Byron Preiss Visual Publications, Inc.

Interior photos: Pages 1, 4, 9, 14 (bottom), 15, 16, 17, 21 (top), 24, 27, and 31 copyright © Boyd Norton; pages 7, 12, 22, 23, and 25 copyright © Evelyn Gallardo; page 13 copyright © Miriam Schlein; page 8 copyright © Robert Lima/Envision; page 14 (top) copyright © Anna E. Zuckerman/Envision; page 28 copyright © Ellen C. Sandberg/Envision; page 29 copyright © Howard Mellowes/Envision; page 18 copyright © John Cancalosi/Peter Arnold, Inc.; page 19 copyright © Dani-Jesque/Bios/Peter Arnold, Inc.; page 20 copyright © Klaus Paysan/Peter Arnold, Inc.; pages 10, 21 (bottom), and 26 copyright © Yann Arthus-Bertrand/Peter Arnold, Inc.

Interior illustrations by Ralph Reese

Special thanks to Kelly Stewart, Sandy Harcourt, Judy Wilson, Jonathan Lanman, and Ana Cerro.

Editor: Ruth Ashby
Associate Editor: Gillian Bucky
Cover design: Ted Mader & Associates
Interior design: Alex Jay/Studio J

10 9 8 7 6 5 4 3 2 1

Library of Congress Cataloging-in-Publication Data
Schlein, Miriam.
    Jane Goodall's animal world. Gorillas/by Miriam Schlein.
    —1st ed.   p.   cm.
    "A Byron Preiss Book."
    Summary: An introduction to gorillas, gentle, shy residents of Africa.
    ISBN 0-689-31473-6
    1. Gorillas—Juvenile literature. [1. Gorillas.] I. Title.
    QL737.P96S36   1990   599.82—dc20
    89-38550   CIP   AC